Healing Pain

Kimberly Renslow

For all those who have felt, the joy, the pain, the tears, and loss of love.

A Wise Woman

How many of you when you look in the street,

See a little old lady dirty but sweet

How many of you see the old lady her wrinkles of age

The traces of tears upon her face

How many look at her tears and realize why she cries

Is it how the world treats her or her own pain

No, it is how the world has become

If she had known sooner things would not be this way

So please take a lesson from the wise lady that begs and pleas

The tears are not for her but for you and me

Angel Fiend

Angel eyes looking through the window

blonde hair flowing down her shoulders

pale snow white skin shutters in the breeze

he let's her in to get warm a blanket soft swallows her tiny body

the crackling fire makes the room glow warm

may I be alone he leaves her there by the fire

working late on his computer screen

silence shattered by a scream

The angel girl he jumps to his feet

A pool of blood from the blanket leaks

He bends to help

The blanket falls revealing her wings

her eyes glaring are fiery gleam

red blood now drips from her teeth

he tries to run in scream a

As her eyes burn brighter

Running to the window he shatters the glass

Cold air breezing through as he turns his back

The wings seep into her skin and the fiery eyes now a clear blue

she is weeping now what do I do.

Dreaming

When you dream what do you dream

When you sleep what do you see

Are you alone, do you fear

How many times do you dream this dream

When you wake what do you scream?

Game Of Life

Play the game the game of life

Sometimes we win and sometimes we lose

You play the game and fight to win

At times you win at times you lose

Everyone hurts with loss

You can have great joy when winning

times are good times are bad

Playing the game we sometimes and up sad

We all play the game

The game of life some people win while others lose.

Let Go

Holding on to anger pain and blame

You need to let it go

Are you the one holding the blade

telling them it's time for them to go home

No holding on to hurt sadness and tears you need to move on

Are you the one who is cheating

telling them you promised to be true

No so let it go

Take your time to cry and yell if it helps

Don't let the hatred of others hold you down

How Do You Make Me Feel

How can you call me baby, then turn around insult me

I wait for you to come home but still I feel alone

How can you say you miss me but never hug your kiss me

It has come to this point where we are just two passing people

I love you are only words said because we don't know what else to say

I tried to tell you the way I feel but you shrug it off like it's no big deal I tried to share my hopes and dreams but hopes and dreams don't pay the bills

The Ghost

Can you feel me there

I know it is hard to see me, but I'm here everyday

I hear your sweet voice

It talks to me I'm here all the time

I can see the tears roll down your cheeks

I can hear you crying yourself to sleep

I wish I could hold you and comfort you in my arms

I want you to know I am here all the time

I want you to know in your bad times and the times you shine

I know how much you love me and that you want me near

I wish you could see that I'm always here.

In My Head

With these thoughts inside my head

many so frightening think of the dead and

still some good thoughts today

Thoughts of being in love but then again

I think I fear my heart being broken

so I do not love with these thoughts inside my head

I start to wonder why I'm not dead.

In My Room

In my room I sit and cry wondering how and wondering why

When things start going good for me there always seems to be a tragedy

I try to stay positive and something comes along and changes it

Why is there so much pain what goodness is there going to

My thoughts are so jumbled and a mess

I really cannot take all the stress

So in my room I sit and cry.

Invisible

I am in love with you

Since the first time we met

It is you I could never forget

I wish you felt this way too

It is you I want to spend my time with

Someday maybe you will see that it is you that completes me

Until then I will wait until you notice me.

Knowing Love

At one time love was so far away lately it's all I feel

Thanks to you I love

You helped me realize life is worth living

So I thank you for helping me see how good it is to let my feelings out

That is good to love and shout it out

That if you have love you have no fears.

Love Hurts

You know I love you this much is true

For some reason I feel so blue

You are always there for me when I cry

That is something I look for in my guy

Still I cannot find some piece of me

These are terms I need to deal with

It hurts so much the pain I feel

I know it's hard for you to understand and you think I have another man.

I Love You I Really Do

I love you I really do

To me what is missing is a big deal

I cannot sleep and I am so sad

When left alone all I do is think of the pain it causes

It drifts into my mind and seeing others achieving my dreams does not help with thing

It is not your fault you do not understand but sometimes I feel you do not even give a damn.

Loving Mother

I know a lady who makes me cry not because she is mean but because her heart is so deep

I weep when I see where her and her children sleep

They have no roof, no floor, no bed

This loving family they sleep in the street

Scraping up what food she can, her children she feeds.

Love Is What I Fear

Love is what I fear do you know how much
I love you

Do you know how much I care

Why are you not home is the question I fear

Have you found another lover

We had some great times talking on the
phone and many nights laughing and joking

We got along so well maybe I did something
is wrong

I guess I'll be all right this would have

happened sooner or later

It is best it happened now only a small piece
of my heart is broken

If only I had not listen to the plans you had made for us believing it someday come true

Now sad and alone at home wondering where I went wrong

I won't count on you to cheer me up or brighten my day.

Much More

The heart does love

Love is a feeling and so much more

Much more than love

Love I think I feel for you

You are the one my heart does love

Love you and so much more

Much more love is felt for you

You are the one that causes the beating of my heart.

Moment To Shine

I have tried to see his point

I have tried to show him mine

I want my moment

I would like to shine

I have tried forget

I have tried to believe

I still would like to be he's free eternity, but

I would like my moment to shine.

Mythical Witch

Silently hiding in plain sight

She wonders if the time is right

To tell him of her ways

hey haven't seen each other for many days

He asked her what was on her mind

Under the blanket she hides as he pulls the blanket away

A shriek she lets out

Mystic words of long ago

He begs and please that it is not so

Angry he turns to leave

He falls to the floor my feet he is shouting

Turning into a fish he flops around she grabs him in her hands

Dropping him in the tank no longer a fish out of water but no longer a man.

New Love To Come

Her dark black hair flows down her back her skin soft and pale as snow

Her voice she's speak softly

She speaks to her love, telling him things of thousands of years ago

She once had love that disappeared, a curse was placed upon him

A serpent he acted and soon he became

She wished he would not have done the

same and

since a snake he acted he became mystic

words before his name

He starts to shrink and slither away

His scaled body slithering out her door

She sits and waits for a new love to come.

No Sound Will Come

He is looking for love but cannot find what he wants

He sees the young girl a bit thin, no she is not right

She needs to be pure but she needs to have bite

He sees her there in a dark corner

Nobody around not a soul in sight

He walks to speak to her

She has the clearest eyes that shine so bright

Her skin is pale and more so in the

moonlight

Reaching for her hand he speaks to her kind of words and understanding

She agrees to come with him and they walk away from the corner, but wait a yelp from the darkness

He runs back and she looks away, a bleeding a man still half alive

I beg you man to run and hide, she did this to me she will do it again.

He grabs the mans hand as he turns to flea

The girl is gone disappeared in the cold

night air

Then suddenly the man starts screaming in the air her blue eyes gleaming

Smiling her sharp teeth now razor white

hitting her mark

He twists and turns trying to scream but no sound will come

His vision gets blurry he falls to the ground

Waking in a bright lit room, thinking what a strange dream

He looks over and sees the girl with the pale
eyes

He tries to scream as she smiles, but no
sound will come.

Open Your Eyes

Something is wrong when mother's do not care

Something is awfully wrong when a father does not care

Something is disturbing when a child walks the streets at night

What is this world coming to

Something is frightening when children are not taught right from wrong

When a child is arrested or encouraged to do as he wishes

When a child takes a gun to school to kill his classmates

When a child is a drug addict

Something is wrong

What are we teaching our children when a child would rather hurt themselves then to deal with the pain

When a child is selling herself to survive on the streets

When a child joins a gang

Why are we not here for the children

This is disturbing, wrong, frustrating, sickening to see children dying

Do their parents not care

Do people not see

Do they just shut their eyes or just not realize what is happening to this world to our children.

To See You Again

I know I should not be sad but it hurts so

You have been there always watching me grow

I know now you are in no pain but I miss you still the same

Maybe you could come back you could be roaming the Earth

While waiting for us to meet again

Wherever you I know you love us still

I know you hear us loving and missing you

It feels as though a piece of my heart has been ripped out and trampled

I have a void because you are gone.

Shared Pain

My mind is in sadness, my heart is in pain

I will never hear you call my name

I do not know why I care for you

I only know I want you near

If ever you need anything at all just call

I will always be there to share my love and care

Simple Questions

If I were to tell you my secret

What would you say

If I asked would you stay

If I cried would you talk me trough it

If I gave you my heart what would you do to it.

So Sad

You are the one who should lift me up when I am blue

Not knock me down and feel useless

You should me feel like the prettiest girl in the world

Not point out my flaws

You should love me for me

So you finally ask why I am sad

But you don't listen or act like you care

I tell you nothing I am tired or some other excuse

You cant handle that it is YOU that makes me sad

I try to follow my dreams with little confidence, that YOU help to breakdown more.

Soul Searching

Soul searching is mind numbing at times

to remember things you would rather forget

I would rather close my eyes and see the good stuff

however lately I close my eyes and I see all the heartache

not just what I have gone through my self but

the pain I made others feel

why do I play back the bad and not noticed the good

I know I have happy moments but

I close my eyes and see the loss

him leaving, her screaming never just a moment of peace

saying goodbye one last time I can't see the smiles on my face.

Surrender

What if the love I gave soon began to fade

what if we no longer cared

what if our love was no longer there

what if your love was to leave unaware that she still cared.

Taken From Me

My friend was taken away

his life now gone taken today

he has not died but still has gone

I shall never see my friend again

somebody told a lie

when I heard this I almost cried

how can you say something that is not true

would you like me to lie to you.

Texas Springtime

The sky is clear and the sun so bright

what a great day you think to yourself

then the clouds roll in and the rain begins to fall

the day turns to gloom the bright fades from the room

then the rain stops and the clouds roll the other way

the sky is clear and bright

you think to yourself I guess I was right.

The Missing Peace

The nights are long since you are gone

the days just pass as if they will forever last

I cannot find sunshine

it seems like happiness is never around

while I sit and cry asking why

my teardrops fall my thoughts float in my mind

surrounding me almost drowning me.

The One

As a recall the first time we met

I remember falling in love

Yet you are just realizing I am the girl for you

even though I always felt this to be true

I wonder what made you see

that there is more to me than what your eyes see.

Time

In my mind I see is there

sharing what no other share

if this is a dream

then do not let me wake

if it is true we should take

all the time that we can take.

The Writer

She is filled with useless knowledge and

always looks the same

she wants to be a writer but

knows nothing of the game

she would love to be the hero but

nobody notices her flying through the air

she longs to find a soul mate but

never leaves home

she moves around sadly and

Is in need of love badly

she watches the hours turn into days

Wondering what her life will become

she wants to have fun but

Is afraid to speak to anyone

she wonders if they hear her when she cries herself to sleep

does anyone realize how deep she let herself sink.

Today

I sit and think about the things I have done

Done many things things that were dumb

dumb things I cannot take back

expecting something wonderful and you just get your feelings hurt hurt is felt when pain is caused

caused by you and cause by me

me I said and think about the things that I have done today.

Voices

Music brings out the voices in my house,

at the same time it brings out the voices in my head

reminds me of bad ideas, death and sorrow

me leaving him and he leaving me

music makes me feel better

even when it drums up the loss and sadness

I feel over again

him dying and her crying music brings out the voices in my her crying music brings out the voices in my head.

What am I to you

If I were a flower

What kind would I be

If I was an animal

How would you see me

If I were a book

What would my title be

If I an ant

Would I be the queen

If I would stop asking questions

Where could this lead

You and I

The stars were shining in the sky

the night was cold like you and I

suddenly a snowflake fell from a cloud above

soon two people fell in love you and I

we went everywhere together that is you and I

soon the snow stopped falling

And the stars stop shining

That was the end of you and I.

Secrets

She has so many secrets that she never will dare tell

She keeps her secrets hidden

burning inside her own private hell

she wishes she could trust someone

so she could set herself free from her own chains.

What are you hiding from

Why hide from your dreams

are you that afraid of failing

yes I dream too big I will never achieve these things

so instead you stop trying you just give up

why allow yourself to sink lower

GET UP GET UP NOW and go after that dream

I cannot I do not have the ability

excuses that is all I see so afraid of letting the world see your greatness

no more worried I will stay invisible and nobody will accept to me

so you need to feel that you are loved and making a difference

I see makes no sense to me

You don't understand

it seems you started this to help yourself so why now do you need the approval of others

I do not know I just want to know that I am helping someone else to see it is okay to feel the way I do.

Can't Let Go

Caring for her lovers she loves them all the same

loving until they hurt her leaving her with pain

even if she left them she shed her tears all day

she gave them pet names and had their song

in her head anyway

then sometimes when she hears it comes running back to the pain

I think she loves being in love more than she will ever say

so when she has the bad points she pushes them away

she likes to hear I love you and don't ever leave me blue

Then she decides she is no longer in love with you

so years down there road she sits and stares and thinks

have I ever loved them and do you really care

as she sits in cries herself to sleep.

You Were There

Sometimes I say thank you and hope that you hear

I have my days I remember how you taught me not to fear

how I need to love myself before I dare love another

nobody else could have helped me the way you brought the true me out

I still try to be true and let the world see

you were the first time I was not afraid to shout

I wasn't afraid to be me and let the real me

out

at time I do get crazy at times a little loud

I know now that even then I should love myself and be proud.

Not mine to keep

We had stolen kisses and

Nights filled with magic

we started as friends and

became a sometime lover

the problem was your heart didn't belong to me

your heart belong to another

I stayed content with what we had.

Ashamed

Feeding myself drugs and liquor it keeps me from being sad

I knew I couldn't keep you, you truly were not mine

so I tried to resist to give a reason for you to not come by

I covered up my sadness I tried not to cry

I knew you never loved me and I knew it all a lie

I tried to stay positive and think about better times

though I keep thinking about when you

were mine

the late night talks and feeling so carefree

Maybe it is because for that brief moment you really belonged to me.

Why

Why can't she be happy

She is all I ever wanted to be

She is my hero

The one I always looked up to

She fights her fights her whole life

Why can't she see

Why can't God let her be happy

I have hated God for doing this to her

She is my best friend

The one who taught me so much about life

I feel like I again let my loved one down.

Taking the blame

At times I crack a smile when I see you in my dreams

then I wake with a tear because I know it is you I am missing

an accident happened you were not even there

do not blame yourself

he knew you cared

then the sickness caught up with her

what else could you do

you know the love she felt for you

all right I understand you taking some of the blame

although you know even with out you the outcome would have been the same

so you take all this pain, you load yourself down with shame

Nobody said it is your fault, nobody but you

It is time to take the sorrow and the tears

Time to wash them away with your damning fears.

Who

If I lost you what would become of me

when you are gone who will be there to help me see

I know it only you that can keep my conscious clean

what am I to do with all of my dreams

who will be there to help me share all of my hopes and all of my fears

if you are no longer here.

Four letter words

I remember when I was little grown ups would say don't use those four letter words like but only with an extra t

My grammie would say shirt but the r would be missing

Once I heard my dad say duck except the d was replaced with a f

I was even told don't say carp when switching the a and r around

However I never realized that D.I.E.T could be a four letter word too.

Healing Heart

I have so much to say but

I don't know where to start I

have to heal myself before

I can love an others heart

I have tried to tell you

I have tried to explain

I fight with myself I take your love in vain

my life has been scrambled for far too long

I have those days that I don't want to go on

when I tell you that I love you do you see my pain.

Don't Do It

Don't be ashamed we all make mistakes

have you learned it was just your fate

don't look back and fear yourself

embrace it all the good the bad

it is what has made you you

be true to yourself and follow your heart

everyone has a low point in life don't make it your everything

relive the joy and banish your fear

be glad you have made it through this many of your years

stay strong, love yourself, and just be happy being you.

Made in the USA
Coppell, TX
27 February 2025

46486520R10037